SUPERGUIDES

BIRDS
OF BRITAIN AND EUROPE

NEIL ARDLEY

KINGFISHER BOOKS

Kingfisher Books, Grisewood & Dempsey Ltd,
Elsley House, 24–30 Great Titchfield Street
London W1P 7AD

This edition published in 1989 by Kingfisher Books.
Material in this book was first published in 1978
in the Kingfisher Guide series.

© Kingfisher Books 1978, 1989

British Library Cataloguing in Publication Data
Ardley, Neil
    Birds of Britain and Europe.
    1. Europe. Birds. Identification
    I. Title II. Series
    598'.07'234

ISBN 0-86272-482-1

Illustrated by Martin Camm

Edited by Janice Lacock
Designed by Millions Design
Printed in Hong Kong

CONTENTS

INTRODUCTION

NAMING BIRDS

Several different features can help you to identify a bird. Its shape, size and pattern of colours are usually enough to be sure of its name, but some birds look rather alike. In these cases, it may help to know the kind of countryside in which the bird is found and in which countries it lives. The way in which it moves, flies and the kind of song that it sings may also help to name a bird.

In this guide, the birds are placed in groups called *orders* or *families*. Each group has a short introduction that describes the general features of the birds in each group and any interesting points about them as a group. On the same page are full-colour paintings of each bird in the group. The paintings show any differences between the male and female, and any changes in colour that occur in different seasons of the year. Where birds appear in more than one form, both are illustrated. If the caption to the painting does not say that the bird is a male or female, then the male and female look alike and cannot be told apart. In the text accompanying each painting is a description of each bird giving its usual English name, its Latin or scientific name (genus and species), its size from the tip of its beak to the end of its tail in centimetres (cm) and inches (in), and a description of its habits and the kind of places in which it is likely to be seen. Any special points of interest are added.

Even amongst a large flock of wildfowl, the male mallard is relatively easy to identify due to his distinctive dark green head and chestnut breast.

IDENTIFYING BIRDS

In order to identify any bird correctly it is important to know what to look for. Study the bird's anatomy so that you can recognize its obvious features. For example, to identify a great tit (page 32), you need only look for a yellow breast and a black central stripe. Remember that the plumage of some birds may change with the seasons.

All the birds illustrated in this book are accompanied by a map showing in which parts of Europe the bird is to be found. In a purple area, the bird may be seen all the year round. In a blue area, it will be found only from late autumn through the winter to early spring. In a pink area, it will be seen only from late spring through summer to early autumn. In a white area, it is not likely to be found at any time, unless migrating between a pink and blue area in spring or autumn.

The birds in this book are those you are most likely to see in Europe. However, birds may sometimes be seen in other places than those mentioned and possibly in other countries than those shown on the maps. Some birds may also look slightly different from their paintings, especially if the light is dim or the birds are juveniles.

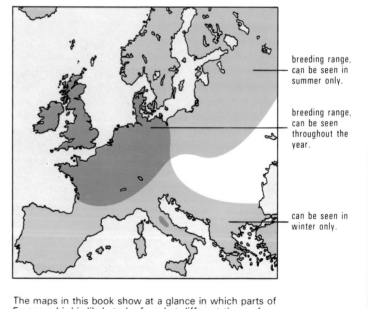

breeding range, can be seen in summer only.

breeding range, can be seen throughout the year.

can be seen in winter only.

The maps in this book show at a glance in which parts of Europe a bird is likely to be found at different times of the year. The pink area indicates the summer range, and blue the winter range. Purple indicates the area where the bird can be seen throughout the year.

THE NAMES OF BIRDS

In the classification of birds, each different kind of bird usually belongs to a separate species and is identified by two Latin names, a *genus* name followed by a *species* name. Similar species of birds belong to the same genus – for example, all the European divers are similar species in the genus *Gavia*. Sometimes three Latin names are given – see the wagtails (page 27) for example. In these cases, the bird is a *subspecies* and belongs to the same species as another subspecies. The two subspecies look slightly different and live in different places, but they may interbreed where they meet. Birds in similar genera (the plural of genus) are grouped together in the same family, and similar families are grouped together in the same order.

This book follows the sequence of orders and families recommended by the British Trust for Ornithology. By grouping birds in this way, similar birds are placed close together, making identification easier. An index of English names at the end of the book (page 40) will help in looking up a particular bird.

WHERE AND WHEN TO SEE BIRDS

You can see birds almost anywhere any time, but different kinds of birds live in different places and the same place may have various birds according to the time of the year. It is interesting to study the features that enable a bird to live in a particular place. For example, woodland birds have very different kinds of feet and beaks from sea birds, because they follow very different ways of life. Few birds can easily live in a wide range of places. However, birds of prey, although mainly scarce nowadays, are to be seen at most kinds of coast and countryside and even in towns.

Some places have greater numbers of birds than others. Every country has natural meeting places for birds where they often gather in huge flocks. Many of these have been made into bird reserves, where the birds are protected so that they can live and nest in safety. At these places, there are often facilities to help birdwatchers to see the birds easily.

STUDYING BIRDS

Looking at birds wherever you happen to find them is an easy way to begin studying them. However, the amount that you will learn about birds will be limited. Few birds will let you approach them, and if you want to spot particular species or observe certain kinds of behaviour, then you will have to search for them. Joining a bird society or club will help you greatly.

A pair of binoculars is an essential aid. Their power should be from 7 × 30 to 10 × 50. Buy the best you can afford but do not get big and heavy binoculars – they are tiring to

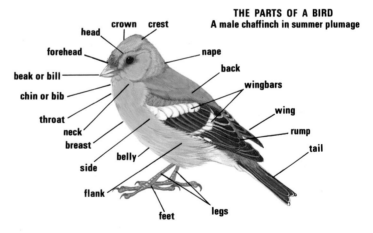

THE PARTS OF A BIRD
A male chaffinch in summer plumage

carry and difficult to hold still. Use binoculars to find birds; by the time you have spotted a bird with the naked eye, raised the binoculars, got the bird in your field of view and focused the binoculars, it will probably have flown away. Be patient and quiet at all times, and wear dark clothes. For close views of birds, you will need to conceal yourself and wait, possibly in a hide, which may be a tent with flaps for windows or perhaps a handy shed.

Always take a notebook and write down your observations. Make notes of the place, date, time, weather, the kind of coutryside or coastline, the birds you see and their behaviour, making drawings if necessary. Taking photographs of birds is not easy, but well worth the effort. A telephoto lens will be needed and the best photographs can be taken from a hide. Electronic flash helps to freeze any action and get sharp close-ups. Recordings of bird song can be made on tape or cassette recorders.

DIVERS AND GREBES

Divers are really at home underwater, where they catch fish and crustaceans. They either dive suddenly from the surface or sink slowly into the water. On land, divers walk clumsily and they normally come ashore only to breed. In winter, all divers become grey-brown above and white below. They can then only be told apart by their size, bill shape and the colours of their backs.

Grebes are elegant water birds with colourful breeding plumage in spring and summer. They feed by diving for fish and other water animals. Although agile in the water, they are not good fliers and may escape danger by partly submerging themselves until only the head remains above water. During courtship, grebes perform dances in which they rush to and fro over the water and freeze in absurd postures.

DIVERS

Order Gaviiformes Family Gaviidae

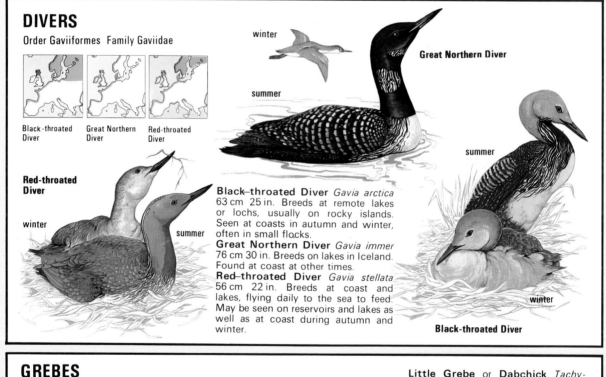

winter

summer

Great Northern Diver

Black-throated Diver

Great Northern Diver

Red-throated Diver

summer

Red-throated Diver

winter

summer

Black–throated Diver *Gavia arctica* 63 cm 25 in. Breeds at remote lakes or lochs, usually on rocky islands. Seen at coasts in autumn and winter, often in small flocks.
Great Northern Diver *Gavia immer* 76 cm 30 in. Breeds on lakes in Iceland. Found at coast at other times.
Red–throated Diver *Gavia stellata* 56 cm 22 in. Breeds at coast and lakes, flying daily to the sea to feed. May be seen on reservoirs and lakes as well as at coast during autumn and winter.

winter

Black-throated Diver

GREBES

Order Podicipediformes Family Podicipitidae

summer

winter

Little Grebe

Great Crested Grebe

Great Crested Grebe *Podiceps cristatus* 46 cm 18 in. Found on inland waters in summer and winter; also at coast in winter. Once hunted for its plumage, it came near to extinction in Britain in 1800s. Recovery mainly due to protection, though building of reservoirs has enabled it to expand.

Great Crested Grebe

Little Grebe or **Dabchick** *Tachybaptus ruficollis* 25 cm 10 in. Found on inland waters in summer and winter; also at coast in winter.

winter

summer

Little Grebe

SHEARWATERS, GANNETS AND CORMORANTS

The fulmar and shearwaters (family Procellariidae) and petrels (family Hydrobatidae) are all ocean birds that normally come ashore only to breed. They may then be seen in colonies on coastal cliffs and islands. The fulmar and the shearwaters are the size of large gulls, but can be told from gulls by the way they glide low over the sea with straight, stiff wings. Shearwaters have narrower wings and thinner, longer bills than the fulmar. Petrels are the smallest European sea birds. They are dark with conspicuous white rumps, and they flutter over the waves.

Gannets (family Sulidae) and cormorants (family Phalacrocoracidae) are the largest European sea birds. Although they have webbed feet, they are not habitual swimmers. They all have different and interesting methods of fishing.

FULMARS, SHEARWATERS AND PETRELS

Order Procellariiformes

Fulmar *Fulmarus glacialis* 46 cm 18 in. Often follows ships, but may come ashore and occupy buildings. Nests in colonies on cliffs. Parents protect the young by ejecting a foul-smelling oily liquid at intruders. There are two colour phases.

Storm Petrel *Hydrobates pelagicus* 15 cm 6 in. Nests in crevices in rocks or stone walls on islands. Can be seen following ships, flitting over the waves summer and autumn. May be seen offshore.

Manx Shearwater *Puffinus puffinus* 36 cm 14 in. Breeds in colonies in burrows on islands and cliff-tops. Does not follow ships. Commonest European shearwater.

Storm Petrel

Fulmar light phase

Manx Shearwater

Manx Shearwater

Fulmar

Storm Petrel

GANNETS AND CORMORANTS

Order Pelecaniformes

Gannet *Sula bassana* 91 cm 36 in. Breeds in summer in vast colonies on cliffs of rocky islands. Winters at sea, but may be seen offshore. May follow ships. Makes spectacular dive into the water to catch fish.

Shag *Phalacrocorax aristotelis* 76 cm 30 in. Identical to cormorant in behaviour, but smaller in size and rarely seen inland. Breeds on rocky cliffs at coast.

Cormorant *Phalacrocorax carbo* 91 cm 36 in. Found at seashores and on inland waters. Flies low over water but settles on surface before diving for fish. Often perches with wings outspread, probably to dry them. Atlantic form is found in Britain, Norway and Iceland and breeds on rocky cliffs. Continental form is found on mainland Europe and nests in trees and bushes.

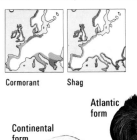

Cormorant   Shag

Gannet

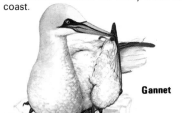

Gannet

Shag

Continental form

Atlantic form

Cormorant

HERONS AND ALLIES

These birds are elegant, long-legged waders. They feed mainly in shallow water, lowering their long necks and bills to catch aquatic animals. Some herons spread their wings while fishing, perhaps to cut out the reflection of the sky. Herons and bitterns (family Ardeidae) and storks (family Ciconiidae) all have straight bills. They can easily be identified in flight because herons and bitterns draw back their heads whereas storks fly with necks outstretched. Grey herons are solitary hunters but breed in tree-top colonies that may number as many as a hundred pairs. The purple heron and the bittern breed among reeds rather than in trees. White storks may nest on trees or roofs.

Order Ciconiiformes

Grey Heron *Ardea cinerea* 91 cm 36 in. The most common and largest European heron. Found on inland waters and at seashore, where it stands motionless in or near water then suddenly darts head down after prey. Also perches in trees, where it usually nests in colonies.

Bittern *Botaurus stellaris* 76 cm 30 in. Hides away and nests among dense reeds. May escape detection by freezing with bill pointing upwards. Foghorn-like booming call may be heard at a great distance.

Purple Heron *Ardea purpurea* 79 cm 31 in. Found in swamps and marshes, where it breeds in colonies among reed-beds and bushes.

Little Egret *Egretta garzetta* 58 in. 23 in. May be found at shallow water of any kind. Usually nests near water. In summer develops hanging plumes, for which it was once hunted.

White Stork *Ciconia ciconia* 102 cm 40 in. Found in marshes, farmland and open country. Nests on buildings, often on special platforms, or in trees near farms and villages. Walks slowly over ground.

Grey Heron   Purple Heron   Little Egret   Bittern   White Stork

Bittern

summer

winter

Little Egret

Purple Heron

Grey Heron

White Stork

WILDFOWL

This group of birds consists of ducks, greese and swans. They are all water birds, and use their webbed feet to swim strongly. The young are born with feathers and can walk and swim soon after hatching. Ducks are usually smaller in size and have shorter necks than geese and swans. In addition, the two sexes have different plumage, although in late summer the drakes (males) moult and for a time resemble the ducks (females). Geese graze mainly on land, and the legs are set forward so that they can walk easily. The sexes are alike. Swans are the largest waterfowl and can be immediately recognized by their long elegant necks, which they lower into the water or to the ground to pull up plants.

DUCKS

Order Anseriformes Family Anatidae

male — female — **Mallard**

female — male — **Gadwall**

female — female — **Teal**

female — female — male — **Pochard**

Pintail — male

male

male — female — **Wigeon**

Pintail *Anas acuta* 63 cm 25 in. Dabbling duck. Prefers inland waters in summer, but coasts in winter.
Pochard *Aythya ferina* 46 cm 18 in. Diving duck. Breeds among reeds, otherwise seen mainly on lakes and at estuaries.

Mallard *Anas platyrhynchos* 58 cm 23 in. Dabbling duck. A very common duck, found on all kinds of inland waters and at coasts and estuaries. Often seen in flocks. Most domestic ducks, though different in colour, are descended from wild mallards.
Teal *Anas crecca* 36 cm 14 in. Dabbling duck. Smallest European duck. Prefers secluded inland waters in summer; spreads to open waters and coast in winter.
Gadwall *Anas strepera* 51 cm 20 in. Dabbling duck. Prefers inland waters.
Wigeon *Anas penelope* 46 cm 18 in. Dabbling duck. Prefers inland waters in summer; spreads to coast in winter, when it may be seen in flocks. May graze on land.

Mallard — Teal — Gadwall

Wigeon — Pochard — Pintail

Tufted Duck *Aythya fuligula* 43 cm 17 in. Diving duck. Often seen on lakes and ponds; also at seashore and estuaries in winter.
Eider *Somateria mollissima* 61 cm 24 in. Diving duck. Most marine of all ducks, seldom found inland. Breeds at seashore, lining nest with soft breast feathers known as eider down.
Common Scoter *Melanitta nigra* 51 cm 20 in. Breeds on islands as well as inland; winters mainly at coast.
Goldeneye *Bucephala clangula* 46 cm 18 in. Diving duck. Nests in tree holes and burrows near fresh water; winters on lakes, rivers and coastal waters. Drakes raise bill in courting display in early spring. Wings whistle in flight.

Red–breasted Merganser *Mergus serrator* 56 cm 22 in. Bill has saw-tooth edges. Breeds near fresh or salt water, hiding nest among rocks or vegetation. Mainly found at coasts in winter.

Shelduck *Tadorna tadorna* 61 cm 24 in. Large goose-like duck. Nests in hollow trees and burrows or among bushes. Winters mainly at coasts, often on mudflats. Sexes almost identical.

female
Common Scoter
male
female
male
Goldeneye
male
female
Tufted Duck
male
female
Eider
Red-breasted Merganser
female
male
Tufted Duck
Eider
Common Scoter
Goldeneye
Red-breasted Merganser
Shelduck
Shelduck
male
female

GEESE

Greylag Goose *Anser anser* 84 cm 33 in. Very common goose. Breeds on moors, marshes, reedy lakes, and offshore islands. Winters in fields, inland and coastal marshes and at estuaries. There are two subspecies, or races. The western race (*A.a. anser*) is found in Iceland, Britain and western Europe; the eastern race (*A.a. rubrirostris*) inhabits eastern Europe. All domestic geese are descended from the greylag goose.
Pink–footed Goose *Anser brachyrhynchus* 68 cm 27 in. Breeds in Arctic; winters inland in fields near water.

Eastern race
Western race
Pink-footed Goose
Greylag Goose

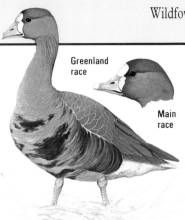

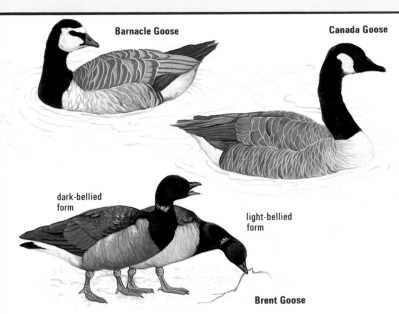

Barnacle Goose

Canada Goose

Greenland race

Main race

dark-bellied form

light-bellied form

Brent Goose

White-fronted Goose

Brent Goose *Branta bernicla* 58 cm 23 in. Winter visitor to coasts and estuaries. Feeds mainly on eel grasses in water, and feeding times depend on tides. There are two subspecies. The light-bellied form (*B.b. hrota*) breeds in Greenland and Spitsbergen, and the dark-bellied form (*B.b. bernicla*) in northern Russia.

Canada Goose *Branta canadensis* 97 cm 38 in. Largest European goose. Introduced from North America to parks. Escaped birds now breed in Britain and Sweden, and may migrate to western Europe for the winter. Wild birds nest on islands in lakes and graze in marshes and fields by lakes and rivers.

White-fronted Goose *Anser albifrons* 71 cm 28 in. Found in same habitat as greylag goose in winter, but breeds in far north. There are two subspecies. The Greenland race (*A.a. flavirostris*) migrates from Greenland to winter in Ireland and western Scotland. The main, or typical, race (*A.a. albifrons*) breeds in northern Russia and winters in the rest of Britain and mainland Europe.

Barnacle Goose *Branta leucopsis* 63 cm 25 in. Winter visitor from Arctic to salt marshes and estuaries and surrounding fields. The odd name comes from a medieval belief that the birds hatch from goose barnacles instead of eggs.

Greylag Goose

White-fronted Goose

Pink-footed Goose

Barnacle Goose

Canada Goose

Brent Goose

SWANS

Mute Swan *Cygnus olor* 152 cm 60 in. Very common. Often found in tame state on park lakes and village ponds and along rivers. Usually nests at banks of rivers and lakes; winters on open waters and at coast.

Whooper Swan *Cygnus cygnus* 152 cm 60 in. Nests in swamps and by lakes in far north; winters along coasts and on lakes and rivers. Its name refers to whooping sound of call.

Mute Swan

Whooper Swan

Bewick's Swan

Bewick's Swan *Cygnus bewickii* 122 cm 48 in. Winter visitors from Arctic. Similar habitat to whooper swan, though prefers larger areas of water in more open country.

Whooper Swan

Mute Swan

Bewick's Swan

BIRDS OF PREY

The birds of prey hunt other animals. Usually they catch live prey on the ground, in the air or in water, but sometimes they eat dead animals. Other birds, such as owls and crows, also feed in these ways, but the birds of prey are different in that they all have sharp claws to grip their victims and hooked beaks to tear them to pieces. Also, unlike most owls, birds of prey hunt by day and not by night. Most of these birds of prey soar through the air, keeping a sharp lookout for prey below and then dropping on an unsuspecting victim. However, vultures land on the ground to feed on carrion (dead animals) and on refuse. Falcons are generally smaller than other birds of prey, and have long, pointed wings and long tails. They are ferocious hunters.

Golden Eagle

VULTURES, EAGLES, BUZZARDS, HAWKS, KITES AND HARRIERS

Family Accipitridae

Golden Eagle *Aquila chrysaetos* 84 cm 33 in. Usually seen soaring above mountain slopes, though may hunt near the ground. May also be found at coasts and in woods and fields. Nests in trees or on rock ledges.

Egyptian Vulture *Neophron percnopterus* 63 cm 25 in. Usually seen in mountains, but comes to rubbish dumps in villages. In Africa, it is well known for its habit of dropping stones on ostrich eggs to break them open.

Red Kite *Milvus milvus* 63 cm 25 in. Usually found in woods, but also among scattered trees. Nests in trees

Honey Buzzard *Pernis apivorus* 53 cm 21 in. Usually found in clearings and at edges of forests and woods. Gets its name from its habit of feeding at the nests of bees and wasps, though for grubs and not for honey. Nests in trees. Colour varies from cream to dark brown.

Buzzard *Buteo buteo* 53 cm 21 in. Found in woods, fields and plains, at coasts and on mountain slopes and hillsides. Often soars, but hunts near the ground. Nests in trees and on rock ledges. Plumage varies from cream to dark brown.

Sparrowhawk *Accipiter nisus* 33 cm 13 in. Usually seen in forests and woods, but also among scattered trees and bushes. Dashes through trees and hops over hedges, hunting small birds. Female is much larger than male. Nests in trees and bushes.

Golden Eagle

Red Kite

Egyptian Vulture

Honey Buzzard

Buzzard

Sparrowhawk

Red Kite

female

male

Buzzard

light form

dark form

Sparrowhawk

Honey Buzzard

Egyptian Vulture

Marsh Harrier *Circus aeruginosus* 51 cm 20 in. Usually seen flying low over swamps and marshes and nearby fields. Nests in reed-beds.
Hen Harrier *Circus cyaneus* 46 cm 18 in. Hunts while flying low over moors, heaths, fields, pasture, marshes and swamps. Makes its nest on the ground.

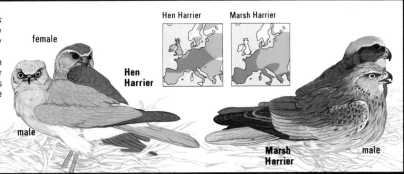

OSPREYS

Family Pandionidae

Osprey *Pandion haliaetus* 56 cm 22 in. Found on lakes and rivers and at coast, where it hunts fish by soaring or hovering high over the water and then plunging in feet-first. Carries fish back to perch near water.

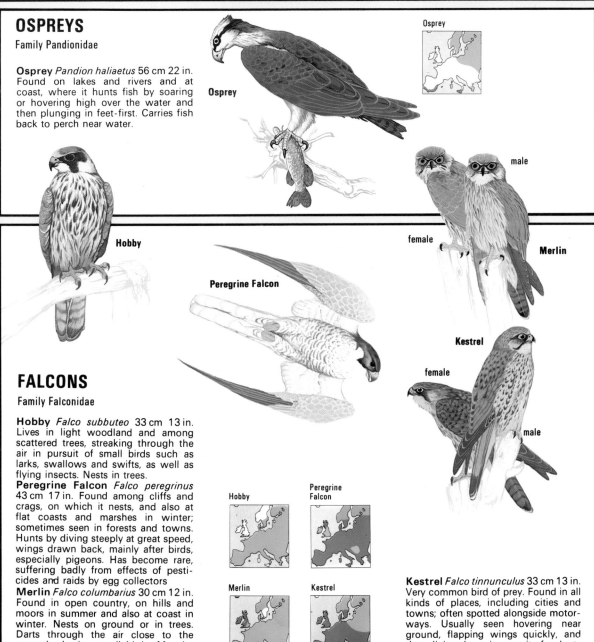

FALCONS

Family Falconidae

Hobby *Falco subbuteo* 33 cm 13 in. Lives in light woodland and among scattered trees, streaking through the air in pursuit of small birds such as larks, swallows and swifts, as well as flying insects. Nests in trees.
Peregrine Falcon *Falco peregrinus* 43 cm 17 in. Found among cliffs and crags, on which it nests, and also at flat coasts and marshes in winter; sometimes seen in forests and towns. Hunts by diving steeply at great speed, wings drawn back, mainly after birds, especially pigeons. Has become rare, suffering badly from effects of pesticides and raids by egg collectors
Merlin *Falco columbarius* 30 cm 12 in. Found in open country, on hills and moors in summer and also at coast in winter. Nests on ground or in trees. Darts through the air close to the ground, chasing small birds. May be seen hovering and perching.

Kestrel *Falco tinnunculus* 33 cm 13 in. Very common bird of prey. Found in all kinds of places, including cities and towns; often spotted alongside motorways. Usually seen hovering near ground, flapping wings quickly, and then diving down in pursuit of rodent and insects.

GAMEBIRDS, CRAKES AND RAILS

These birds are plump in shape, rather like chickens. They rarely fly very far or high and prefer to run or hide from danger, only taking to the air at the last moment. They spend most of their time on the ground rooting for seeds and insects, and they also nest on the ground. They are called gamebirds because most of them are hunted for sport, although hunting is forbidden when the birds are nesting and raising their young. Grouse live in cold places, and their legs and sometimes their feet are covered with feathers for warmth. Unlike grouse, partridges and pheasants have bare legs and feet and are not found in cold places. Brightly coloured pheasants from other parts of the world are seen in parks. Crakes and rails (family Rallidae) are mainly water birds. They are small to medium in size, chunky in shape and have long legs.

GROUSE
Family Tetraonidae

Black Grouse *Lyrurus tetrix* Male 53 cm 21 in; female 41 cm 16 in. Found on moors, in woods, among scattered trees and in fields. In spring, groups gather at courting grounds and the males display themselves before the females, spreading their wings and raising their white tail feathers in a fan shape.

Capercaillie *Tetrao urogallus* Male 86 cm 34 in; female 61 cm 24 in. Lives among fir trees on hills and mountains. Male raises tail in a fan when courting female.

Willow Grouse *Lagopus lagopus* 38 cm 15 in. Found on moors, often living among heather and scattered bushes. Plumage changes from white in winter to brown and white in summer, helping to hide bird among winter snow and summer plants.

Red Grouse *Lagopus lagopus scoticus* 38 cm 15 in. A variety of willow grouse found only in the British Isles. No colour change takes place because snow does not always fall in winter. Lives among heather on moors, but also found in fields in winter.

Ptarmigan *Lagopus mutus* 36 cm 14 in. Found on high mountain slopes, usually above tree level. Plumage changes from brown and white in summer to grey and white in autumn and pure white in winter. In this way, it always matches its surroundings and cannot easily be spotted by an eagle or a fox.

14

PARTRIDGES AND PHEASANTS

Family Phasianidae

Red-legged Partridge *Alectoris rufa* 34 cm 13½ in. Found on moors, and in fields and low treeless hills, often in dry and stony places. Looks like rock partridge, but lives in different countries.
Partridge *Perdix perdix* 30 cm 12 in. Seen mainly in fields, but also on moors and heaths and in marshes, sand dunes and low treeless hills.

Quail *Coturnix coturnix* 18 cm 7 in. The smallest European game bird, and the only one that migrates. Hides among grass and crops.
Pheasant *Phasianus colchicus* Male 84 cm 33 in; female 58 cm 23 in. Often seen in fields, especially in winter; also in woods and marshes. Pattern of male varies; for example some have white neck-ring while others do not.

Red-legged Partridge

male

female

Quail

male

female

Partridge

Pheasant

male

female

CRAKES AND RAILS

Order Gruiformes

Water Rail *Rallus aquaticus* 28 cm 11 in. Usually hides among reeds in marshes and ponds, and nests on concealed platform of reeds built above water. Likely to come into the open during cold weather.

Moorhen *Gallinula chloropus* 33 cm 13 in. Lives on ponds, lakes and streams, bobbing its head up and down as it swims to and fro and sometimes diving for food. Often seen in parks. Nests in reeds, bushes and trees, usually near the water. Often feeds on grassy banks and in nearby fields.
Coot *Fulica atra* 38 cm 15 ih. Found on lakes, reservoirs and rivers, and in parks. Also at coast in winter. Prefers larger stretches of water than does moorhen, and dives more often. Usually seen in groups, with the birds always quarrelling. Nests in reeds and plants at water's edge.

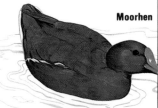

Moorhen

Coot

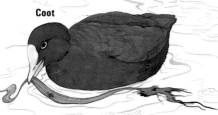

Moorhen

Coot

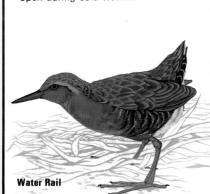

Water Rail

Water Rail

WADERS

Waders live at the seashore and in marshes. They have long legs so that they can walk in shallow water. Plovers can be told from almost all other waders by their short beaks. They probe in soil, mud and sand, both at the seashore and inland, for worms, grubs and shellfish. They often run about, stopping to bob their heads or tilt them at an angle, as if listening for something. All plovers nest on the ground. Many protect their young from enemies by pretending to have a broken wing and luring them away from the nest. Sandpipers may be found inland at damp places as well as at the seashore, and they usually nest on the ground. Flocks of several different kinds of sandpipers can often be seen feeding together at the shore, poking their bills into the water, mud or sand to find shellfish and worms. All sandpipers have long bills, but the length varies. This is because the birds probe at different depths according to the type of food they live on. Avocets are the most elegant wading birds with their stilt-like legs and long, thin beaks.

PLOVERS
Family Charadriidae

Lapwing, Peewit or **Green Plover** *Vanellus vanellus* 30 cm 12 in. Very common plover. Found in fields and marshes and on moors; also at coast in winter. Usually in large flocks.
Ringed Plover *Charadrius hiaticula* 19 cm 7½ in. Usually found on sandy and stony beaches, sometimes inland.
Little Ringed Plover *Charadrius dubius* 15 cm 6 in. Lives on sandy or stony shores of lakes and rivers, and in old gravel pits.
Kentish Plover *Charadrius alexandrinus* 15 cm 6 in. Found at seashore, on sandy or stony beaches.
Grey Plover *Pluvialis squatarola* 28 cm 11 in. Found on mudflats and sandy beaches.
Golden Plover *Pluvialis apricaria* 28 cm 11 in. Nests on moors in summer. In winter, also found in fields and at seashore, usually with lapwings.
Turnstone *Arenaria interpres* 23 cm 9 in. Found at coast, usually on rocky and stony shores. Gets name from its habit of turning over stones, shells and seaweed when looking for food.

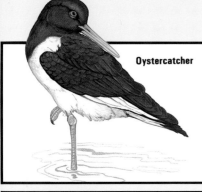

Oystercatcher

OYSTERCATCHERS

Family Haematopodidae

Oystercatcher *Haematopus ostralegus* 43 cm 17 in. The only European member of its family. Seen at seashore, prising shellfish open with its chisel-like beak. Also probes for food in mud. May also be found inland on moors and by lakes and rivers.

Oystercatcher

SANDPIPERS

Family Scolopacidae

Woodcock

Curlew

Snipe

Snipe *Gallinago gallinago* 27 cm 10½ in. Hides away in marshes, bogs and damp meadows. Flies away with zigzag flight when disturbed. Often dives from sky, making a drumming noise with its tail.

Woodcock *Scolopax rusticola* 36 cm 14 in. Hides away among damp woodland. Most likely to be seen at dawn or dusk flying through the trees or in circles above the trees.

Curlew *Numenius arquata* 56 cm 22 in. Nests on moors and in marshes, damp meadows and sand dunes. In winter, also seen on mudflats at seashore.

Black–tailed Godwit *Limosa limosa* 41 cm 16 in. Nests in damp meadows and on boggy land. In winter, also seen on mudflats and in marshes.

Bar–tailed Godwit *Limosa lapponica* 38 cm 15 in. Nests in marshes in Arctic and migrates to spend winter at seashore.

Common Sandpiper *Tringa hypoleucos* 20 cm 8 in. Nests beside streams, rivers and lakes, usually in hills. In winter, also seen at seashore. Bobs its tail and nods its head as it wades.

Green Sandpiper *Tringa ochropus* 23 cm 9 in. Nests in swamps in woodland. Winters in marshes and on lakes and rivers, seldom at coast.

Snipe

Woodcock

Curlew

Black-tailed Godwit

Bar-tailed Godwit

Common Sandpiper

Green Sandpiper

summer

winter

Bar-tailed Godwit

winter

Green Sandpiper

winter

summer

Black-tailed Godwit

Common Sandpiper

Redshank

Greenshank

summer   winter   winter   summer

Sanderling

Male displaying
in summer

Spotted Redshank

summer

Knot

winter

summer

winter

summer

winter

**Purple
Sandpiper**

winter

Ruff

male (winter)

female

Redshank *Tringa totanus* 28 cm 11 in.
Nests among grass in meadows and
inland and coastal marshes and on
moors and heaths. In winter, usually
found at seashore.
Spotted Redshank *Tringa erythropus*
30 cm 12 in. Nests in far north and
migrates to spend winter at seashore
and in marshes.
Greenshank *Tringa nebularia* 30 cm
12 in. Nests on ground on moors or in
forests, usually near water. In winter,
seen at seashore and on inland waters.

Knot *Calidris canutus* 25 cm 10 in.
A winter visitor from the Arctic. Seen
at mudflats along seashores, often in
flocks. Birds in summer plumage may
be seen in spring and autumn.
Purple Sandpiper *Calidris maritima*
20 cm 8 in. Found at rocky shores and
harbours in winter. Nests among low
plants in far north. Back has purple
gloss, but this can be seen only in
bright light.
Sanderling *Calidris alba* 20 cm 8 in.
Seen in winter at sandy beaches,
racing about as if chasing the waves.
Migrates to Arctic to breed.
Ruff *Philomachus pugnax* Male: 30 cm
12 in; female: 23 cm 9 in. Nests on
moors and in marshes and meadows;
also found beside rivers and lakes
in winter. In late spring and early
summer, the males attract the females
by raising a beautiful ruff of feathers
around the neck. The colour of the
ruff varies greatly. The female is also
known as a reeve.

Redshank	Spotted Redshank	Greenshank	Knot	Purple Sandpiper	Sanderling	Ruff

AVOCETS

Family Recurvirostridae

Avocet *Recurvirostra avosetta* 43 cm
17 in. Nests in marshes at or near
coast; spends winter at estuaries.
Best seen at bird reserves. Beak
curves upwards so that the end skims
surface of water.

Avocet

Avocet

SKUAS AND AUKS

All these birds are sea birds. Skuas often chase other sea birds and make them drop a fish they have just captured or even half eaten! The skua then swoops down to catch its stolen meal before it hits the water below. Auks look and behave very much like penguins. They dive for fish and chase them underwater, using their wings like oars and their feet like a rudder. On land, they sit up and waddle about. They spend most of the year at sea and only come ashore to breed. Unlike penguins, they can fly.

SKUAS

Family Stercorariidae

Great Skua *Stercorarius skua* 58 cm 23 in. Nests among grass or heather on moors, and spends winter out to sea. May be seen at coast on migration in spring and autumn.
Arctic Skua *Stercorarius parasiticus* 46 cm 18 in. Lives in similar places to great skua. The neck, breast and underparts may be light, dark or any shade between.

Great Skua diving

dark form

light form

Great Skua

Arctic Skua

Great Skua　　Arctic Skua

AUKS

Family Alcidae

Razorbill *Alca torda* 41 cm 16 in. Breeds in colonies on cliff ledges at coast, often with guillemots. Spends winter out to sea, although storms may force it back to shore.

winter

summer

Black Guillemot

Razorbill

summer

summer

Guillemot

winter

Black Guillemot *Cepphus grylle* 33 cm 13 in. Nests in holes and crevices on rocky shores and sea cliffs, but not in large colonies. Stays near shore in winter.

summer

winter

Puffin

Puffin *Fratercula arctica* 30 cm 12 in. Nests in colonies in burrows in steep slopes by sea. May run down slope to get into the air. Can hold several fish at once in its parrot-like beak. Spends winter far out to sea and seldom blown ashore.
Guillemot *Uria aalge* 41 cm 16 in. Breeds in large colonies on cliff ledges at coast and on offshore islands. The guillemot's egg is laid on bare rock and is pear-shaped, so that it rolls in a circle and not over the edge if knocked. Spends winter out to sea, but may be driven ashore by gales.

Razorbill　　Puffin

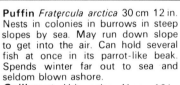

Guillemot

Black Guillemot

GULLS AND TERNS

These two kinds of sea birds are easy to tell apart. Gulls have broad wings and fan-shaped tails, and their beaks are usually heavy with a hooked tip. They can be seen in flocks at the seashore and at harbours, constantly making mewing cries as they wheel to and fro in the air. To feed, they settle on the water and seize some floating waste or dip their heads under the water to catch a fish. Gulls also fly inland, especially in winter. They can be seen looking for food on rubbish tips and newly ploughed fields. They nest in colonies on the ground and on cliffs. Young gulls look brown and white until they are about four years old.

Terns have slender wings and forked tails, and sharp beaks that often point downwards during flight. They fly low and sometimes hover over the water, then dive to catch a fish. Terns can be seen at the seashore and at inland marshes and lakes. They nest on the ground in colonies, and may attack any person or animal approaching too close to the nest. Terns migrate great distances to spend the winter far to the south.

Family Laridae

Great Black–backed Gull *Larus marinus* 68 cm 27 in. Usually seen at rocky coasts and offshore islands; may be seen inland, especially in winter. Often feeds on eggs and young of other sea birds.

Lesser Black–backed Gull *Larus fuscus* 53 cm 21 in. Often seen at seashore and harbours and also inland. The British form (*Larus fuscus graellsii*) has a lighter back than the Scandinavian form (*Larus fuscus fuscus*), which looks like a small great black-backed gull.

Herring Gull *Larus argentatus* 56 cm 22 in. A very common gull, seen both at the coast and inland.

Common Gull *Larus canus* 41 cm 16 in. Found at coast and inland. In spite of its name, it is not the most numerous gull.

Glaucous Gull *Larus hyperboreus* 71 cm 28 in. Nests in Iceland and in Arctic; seen at coasts and harbours in winter, rarely inland. Preys on eggs and small birds.

Little Gull *Larus minutus* 28 cm 11 in. Gets its name because it is noticeably smaller than other gulls. Nests in marshes and swamps, but seen at coast and inland at other times. Catches insects in flight.

Great Black-backed Gull

Scandinavian form

British form

Lesser Black-backed Gull

Little Gull in winter

summer

Little Gull

Glaucous Gull

Herring Gull

Common Gull

Great Black-backed Gull

Lesser Black-backed Gull

Glaucous Gull

Herring Gull

Common Gull

Little Gull

Black–headed Gull *Larus ridibundus* 38 cm 15 in. A very common gull, often seen inland. Nests in marshes, on moors, and by lakes and rivers. At other times found at coasts and harbours, and in fields and towns. Eats anything, including fish, worms, flying insects and even garbage. Badly named, as other gulls have black heads and the head is dark brown but goes white in winter!

Kittiwake *Rissa tridactyla* 41 cm 16 in. Nests in colonies on cliff ledges and also on buildings in coastal towns. Usually spends winter far out to sea.

Black Tern *Chlidonias niger* 24 cm 9½ in. Builds floating nest on lakes and marsh pools; may be seen at coast during migration in spring and autumn. Chases insects in air; rarely dives into water.

Common Tern *Sterna hirundo* 36 cm 14 in. Nests on beaches, among sand dunes, in coastal swamps, on offshore islands and by lakes. Often seen flying along seashore and diving for fish.

Arctic Tern *Sterna paradisaea* 36 cm 14 in. Found in same kinds of places as common tern, but less likely inland. May migrate as far south as the Antarctic to spend the winter.

Roseate Tern *Sterna dougallii* 38 cm 15 in. Nests on rocky islands and beaches, sometimes with common terns and arctic terns; seldom found inland.

Little Tern *Sterna albifrons* 24 cm 9½ in. Nests mainly on sandy and stony beaches, but sometimes at places inland.

Sandwich Tern *Sterna sandvicensis* 41 cm 16 in. Nests in colonies on sandy and stony beaches and also on offshore islands. Rarely found inland. Named after Sandwich in Kent, where a famous colony once existed.

Kittiwake

Black-headed Gull

summer

Black-headed Gull in winter

Black Tern

Common Tern

Roseate Tern

Little Tern

Arctic Tern

Sandwich Tern

Black-headed Gull

Black Tern

Common Tern

Arctic Tern

Kittiwake

Roseate Tern

Little Tern

Sandwich Tern

PIGEONS, DOVES AND CUCKOOS

Pigeons and doves have plump bodies, small heads and short legs. They can all fly very fast, and people raise pigeons for racing. They are likely to be seen waddling about on the ground, pecking for food. Unlike other birds which have to tip their heads back to get water to flow down their throats, pigeons and doves can suck up water to drink.

Cuckoos are famous for laying their eggs in the nests of other birds and leaving the hosts to bring up the young cuckoos. They get their name from the unmistakable call that heralds their arrival in spring.

PIGEONS AND DOVES

Order Columbiformes

Woodpigeon

Rock Dove

Stock Dove

Collared Dove

Turtle Dove

Stock Dove   Rock Dove   Woodpigeon   Turtle Dove   Collared Dove

Stock Dove *Columba oenas* 33 cm 13 in. Found in woods and on farmland; may also be seen in parks and at cliffs and sand dunes along coast.
Rock Dove *Columba livia* 33 cm 13 in. Lives at rocky coasts and on mountains, and nests in caves and on cliff ledges. The pigeons that can be seen in city squares and parks, as well as the pigeons that people raise for racing, are all descended from the wild rock dove. Some of these pigeons still look like their wild ancestor, but many now have different plumage. The pigeons are interbreeding with the rock doves, and the wild birds are slowly disappearing.
Collared Dove *Streptopelia decaocto* 30 cm 12 in. Usually found in towns or close to houses and farms. Nests on buildings or in trees nearby. Until 1930, collared doves lived in Asia and south-east Europe. Then they began to spread to the north-west. They reached Britain in 1955 and have recently moved on to Iceland.
Woodpigeon *Columba palumbus* 41 cm 16 in. Found in woods and on farmland, and also in parks and gardens. Often seen in flocks containing stock doves and domestic pigeons.
Turtle Dove *Streptopelia turtur* 28 cm 11 in. Found in spring and summer in light woods and among scattered trees and bushes; also on farmland and in parks and gardens.

CUCKOOS

Order Cuculiformes Family Cuculidae

Cuckoo *Cuculus canorus* 33 cm 13 in. Found in woodland, open ground with scattered trees and bushes, and on moors. Only the male makes 'cuckoo' call; female has babbling call. The female cuckoo lays several eggs, one each in the nests of other birds. Small birds are chosen, such as meadow pipits and robins, but each female cuckoo always uses nests of the same species. When it hatches, the young cuckoo pushes out any other eggs and nestlings, but its adopted parents continue to feed it, driven by instinct.

Cuckoo

grey form (adult)

red form (young)

Cuckoo

OWLS

Owls are not often seen because they usually come out only at night to hunt mice and other small animals. However, their unusual hoot gives a clue to their whereabouts, and in the daytime small birds may gather around a sleeping owl and try to make it fly away. Owls have large eyes set in front of their heads to help them spot their prey in the dark. They also fly without a sound. Owls nest in holes in trees or the ground, or sometimes in buildings. There are two groups: barn owls (family Tytonidae) and all other owls (family Strigidae).

OWLS
Order Strigiformes

Barn Owl *Tyto alba* 36 cm 14 in. Found on farmland and in marshes but also occupies unused buildings, such as barns and church towers, and ruins. Most likely to be seen at dusk. Two forms occur, a white-breasted form (*Tyto alba alba*) in south and west Europe, and a buff-breasted form (*Tyto alba guttata*) in north and east Europe.

Scops Owl *Otus scops* 19 cm 7½ in. Found among trees, often near buildings, as well as in ruins. Rarely seen in daytime. Like other owls, has ear tufts that are not ears but merely tufts of head feathers.

Little Owl *Athene noctua* 23 cm 9 in. Found among scattered trees, in fields and on open ground, often near buildings. May be seen in daytime, bobbing and turning its head as it perches on a post or branch.

Tawny Owl *Strix aluco* 38 cm 15 in. A very common owl. Lives in woods and also in parks and gardens. Usually hunts by night, but may be seen sleeping in tree during daytime, when it is sometimes bothered by small birds. Colour may vary from brown to grey.

Long–eared Owl *Asio otus* 36 cm 14 in. Sleeps in woods, especially in fir trees, by day and comes out to hunt, often over open ground, at dusk. May be seen sleeping in groups in winter.

Short–eared Owl *Asio flammeus* 38 cm 15 in. Seen hunting over moors, marshes and open ground during daytime and at dusk. Ear tufts are very short, often invisible.

dark-breasted form

Barn Owl

light-breasted form

Short-eared Owl

Scops Owl

brown form

Tawny Owl

grey form

Long-eared Owl

Little Owl

Barn Owl	Scops Owl	Little Owl	Tawny Owl	Long-eared Owl	Short-eared Owl

NIGHTJARS, WOODPECKERS AND RELATIVES

This group of birds contains a wide range of different birds. Swifts are masters of the air and are usually seen in flocks, wheeling high in the sky at great speed. They may spend weeks in the air without coming down as they catch flying insects for food and can sleep in flight. Kingfishers (family Alcedinidae), hoopoes (family Upupidae) and roller (family Coraciidae) are the most colourful and spectacular birds to be seen in Europe. Woodpeckers are often heard before being seen. Their sharp beaks make a loud rat-a-tat as they chisel into the bark of a tree in search of insects. They also dig out holes for nesting.

male

female

NIGHTJARS

Order Caprimulgiformes

Family Caprimulgidae

Nightjar *Caprimulgus europaeus* 28 cm 11 in. Lives in woods, among bracken in clearings and on hillsides, on moors and in sand dunes. Unless disturbed, it is very difficult to spot. Sleeps during the day and hunts for insects at night. Lays eggs on the ground.

Nightjar

Nightjar

SWIFTS

Order Apodiformes Family Apodidae

Swift

Swift

Swift *Apus apus* 16 cm 6½ in. Nests in holes in trees, crevices in cliffs, and under the eaves of buildings. Often to be seen at dusk, dashing around rooftops in noisy flocks. May be seen with swallows (page 26), but can easily be recognized by dark underparts and shallow forked tail.

KINGFISHERS AND RELATED BIRDS

Order Coraciiformes

Kingfisher *Alcedo atthis* 16 cm 6½ in. Seen by rivers and lakes, perching on a branch beside the water or darting down to plunge for a fish. May also be seen at coast in winter.

Roller *Coracias garrulus* 30 cm 12 in. Found in open country with scattered trees and in woods. Nests in hole in tree or bank. Often seen perching and then swooping down to catch insects and other small animals. Gets its name from the way it rolls over in flight to attract a mate during the spring courtship.

Hoopoe *Upupa epops* 28 cm 11 in. Seen among scattered trees and in woods; sometimes in parks and gardens. Nests in hole in tree or wall. Often seen perching, usually with its crest down. Named after its call.

Kingfisher

Roller

Hoopoe

Kingfisher

crest up

Hoopoe

crest down

Roller

WOODPECKERS
Order Piciformes Family Picidae

Wryneck

male

**Great Spotted
Woodpecker**

female

Wryneck *Jynx torquilla* 16 cm 6½ in. Lives in light woodland, and in open country with scattered trees, bushes and hedges, orchards, parks and gardens. Does not look like a woodpecker and does not chisel into bark. Often feeds on ground and nests in existing holes, including nest-boxes. Gets its name from the way it can turn its head round.

Green Woodpecker *Picus viridis* 30 cm 12 in. Found in woods and forests, usually of broad-leaved trees, and in open country with scattered trees. Also seen on ground, feeding at anthills.

Grey–headed Woodpecker *Picus canus* 25 cm 10 in. Found in same places as green woodpecker. Often drums in spring, unlike green woodpecker.

Great Spotted Woodpecker *Dendrocopos major* 23 cm 9 in. Found in woods and forests of all kinds, and also in parks and gardens. Comes to bird tables.

Middle Spotted Woodpecker *Dendrocopos medius* 20 cm 8 in. Lives in woods and forests, though seldom among fir trees. Usually stays high up in trees.

Lesser Spotted Woodpecker *Dendrocopos minor* 15 cm 6 in. Lives in same places as middle spotted woodpecker, but may also be found in parks and orchards. Smallest European woodpecker.

There are over 200 kinds of woodpeckers all over the world, except Australia and Madagascar. Nest cavities made by woodpeckers can be up to 50 cm (20 in) deep and have entrance holes up to 8 cm (3 in) across. The entrance hole is at the top of the nest cavity.

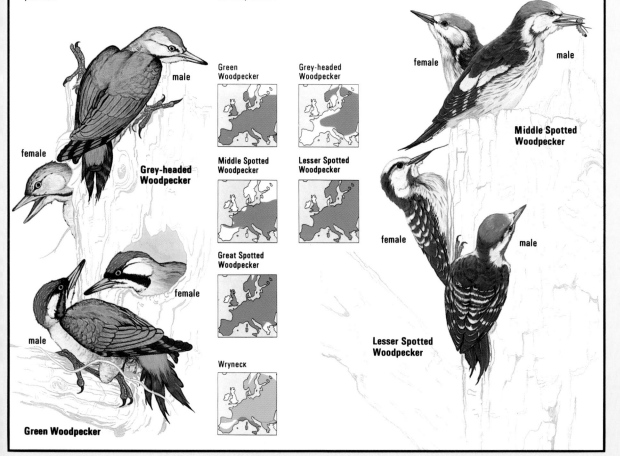

male

female

Grey-headed Woodpecker

female

male

Green Woodpecker

Green Woodpecker

Grey-headed Woodpecker

Middle Spotted Woodpecker

Lesser Spotted Woodpecker

Great Spotted Woodpecker

Wryneck

female

male

Middle Spotted Woodpecker

female

male

Lesser Spotted Woodpecker

LARKS, SWALLOWS, PIPITS AND WAGTAILS

All the birds on pages 26–39 belong to the order Passeriformes and are classed as perching birds and songbirds. They are to be found everywhere. Their feet have three toes in front and a long one behind, which enables them to perch easily. Many, but not all, can sing well.

Larks are most often seen in the air, singing strongly. Swallows and martins fly very fast, often near the ground, twisting and turning in the air as they chase flying insects. Pipits and wagtails are small birds that spend most of their time on the ground in search of insects. Pipits look like several other streaky brown ground birds, but they can be recognized by their narrow beaks and slender bodies. Wagtails have long tails, which they wag up and down all the time.

LARKS
Family Alaudidae

Woodlark   Skylark

Skylark

Woodlark

Woodlark *Lullula arborea* 15 cm 6 in. Found in fields and open country, often among scattered trees and bushes, and at woodland edges. Often flies in circle while singing; also sings while perched.

Skylark *Alauda arvensis* 18 cm 7 in. Found in all kinds of open country – moors, marshes, fields and sand dunes. Rises straight up into air and may hover while singing.

SWALLOWS AND MARTINS
Family Hirundinidae

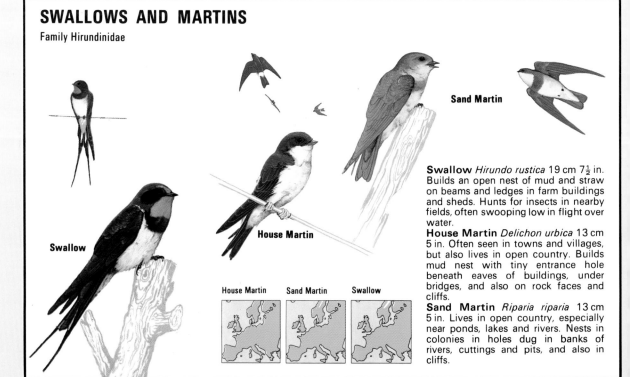

Sand Martin

Swallow

House Martin

House Martin   Sand Martin   Swallow

Swallow *Hirundo rustica* 19 cm 7½ in. Builds an open nest of mud and straw on beams and ledges in farm buildings and sheds. Hunts for insects in nearby fields, often swooping low in flight over water.

House Martin *Delichon urbica* 13 cm 5 in. Often seen in towns and villages, but also lives in open country. Builds mud nest with tiny entrance hole beneath eaves of buildings, under bridges, and also on rock faces and cliffs.

Sand Martin *Riparia riparia* 13 cm 5 in. Lives in open country, especially near ponds, lakes and rivers. Nests in colonies in holes dug in banks of rivers, cuttings and pits, and also in cliffs.

PIPITS AND WAGTAILS

Family Motacillidae

Meadow Pipit

Tree Pipit

Rock Pipit

male

Yellow Wagtail

summer

winter

White Wagtail

female

winter

summer

Pied Wagtail

female

Grey Wagtail

male (winter)

male (summer)

Meadow Pipit | Tree Pipit

Rock Pipit | White Wagtail

Pied Wagtail | Grey Wagtail

Yellow Wagtail

Meadow Pipit *Anthus pratensis* 15 cm 6 in. Found in all kinds of open country — moors, fields, dunes, grassy slopes — and in winter in marshes and along rivers, often at the coast. Makes its nest on the ground hidden among low plants. May be seen and heard singing as it makes short flights rising from and returning to ground.

Tree Pipit *Anthus trivialis* 15 cm 6 in. Lives in light woods and clearings and among scattered trees and bushes. Nests among low plants on ground. May be seen and heard singing in short spiral flight rising from a perch.

Rock Pipit *Anthus spinoletta petrosus* 16 cm 6½ in. Belongs to same species as water pipit, but lives at coast, often among rocks. Nests in rock crevices.

White Wagtail *Motacilla alba alba* 18 cm 7 in. Often found in open country, usually near water, and also on farms and in villages and towns. Nests in holes and on ledges among rocks and on buildings. In winter, large groups sleep on buildings and in trees in cities and towns.

Pied Wagtail *Motacilla alba yarrellii* 18 cm 7 in. Form of white wagtail found mainly in British Isles. Lives and nests in same places as the white wagtail.

Grey Wagtail *Motacilla cinerea* 18 cm 7 in. In spring and summer, found by streams and rivers, mostly in hills and mountains, where it nests in hole in wall or rock beside water. In winter, moves to lowland rivers and lakes, sewage farms and coast.

Yellow Wagtail *Motacilla flava* 16 cm 6½ in. Found in marshes and fields, usually near water. Nests on the ground, among grass or crops. Several forms with different head patterns and different names live in Europe. They all have their own regions but where these meet, intermediate forms may be seen. In southern Scandinavia and central Europe, the blue-headed wagtail (*Motacilla flava flava*) is found. Britain is the home of the yellow wagtail (*Motacilla flava flavissima*). The Spanish wagtail (*Motacilla flava iberiae*) lives in Spain, Portugal and southern France. In Italy and Albania, the ashy-headed wagtail (*Motacilla flava cinereocapilla*) is found, and the blackheaded wagtail (*Motacilla flava feldegg*) lives in south-east Europe. Each kind may sometimes stray from its own region.

THRUSHES AND CHATS

This large family of birds contains several birds that are well known as visitors to gardens. They feed mainly on fruits, berries and insects, but are often to be seen looking for worms. Thrushes are medium-sized birds and have slender bills, long wings and tails. The young birds are all spotted but some, such as the male blackbird, lose their spots as they mature. Thrushes have beautiful songs, which they seem to perform just for the pleasure of singing. Nightingales, in particular, are renowned for their melodious singing.

Originally most of the thrushes and chats were woodlands birds, but some, especially the robin and blackbird, are now familiar sights in suburban gardens. They have been known to build their nests in man-made objects such as flowerpots, discarded kettles and brooms. Many thrushes and chats are migrants.

Family Turdidae

Mistle Thrush *Turdus viscivorus* 28 cm 11 in. Found in woods, farmland, parks and gardens; also on moors in winter. Nests in trees.

Fieldfare *Turdus pilaris* 25 cm 10 in. Found in woods and, in northern Europe, in parks and gardens. Nests in trees or on buildings. In winter spreads in flocks to fields and open country with hedges and scattered trees.

Song Thrush *Turdus philomelos* 23 cm 9 in. Often seen in woods and orchards, among scattered bushes and hedges, and in parks and gardens. May be seen on lawns cocking its head to one side, as if listening but in fact looking for a worm. Drops snails on to a stone (called an anvil) to break open their shells. Nests in trees, bushes and hedges, and also on buildings.

Redwing *Turdus iliacus* 20 cm 8 in. Found in woods and, in northern Europe, in parks and gardens. In fields and open country in winter. Nests in trees and on the ground.

Ring Ouzel *Turdus torquatus* 24 cm 9½ in. Lives on moors and mountain slopes, often where there are scattered trees and bushes. Nests among low plants or on rock ledges or walls.

Blackbird *Turdus merula* 25 cm 10 in. Very often seen in woods, orchards, hedges, parks and gardens; also in fields in winter. Nests in trees, bushes or hedges, on the ground or on buildings. Some blackbirds are albino birds that have white patches or may even be entirely white.

Fieldfare

Song Thrush

Mistle Thrush

Redwing

Ring Ouzel

male

female

male

female

Blackbird

Mistle Thrush   Fieldfare   Song Thrush   Redwing   Ring Ouzel   Blackbird

Wheatear *Oenanthe oenanthe* 15 cm 6 in. Lives in open country, from high moors and grassy hillsides down to coasts. Nests in holes in ground or in walls and rocks.

Stonechat *Saxicola torquata* 13 cm 5 in. Found on moors, on headlands at coast and on rough ground with bushes, especially gorse. Often seen perching, flicking its tail up and down. The nest is hidden in a bush or among grass.

Whinchat *Saxicola rubetra* 13 cm 5 in. Lives in similar places to stonechat, but also likes grassy areas and fields. Behaves in same way as stonechat.

Redstart *Phoenicurus phoenicurus* 14 cm 5½ in. Found in woods and among scattered trees; also in parks and gardens. Constantly flicks its tail up and down. Nests in holes in trees and walls.

Black Redstart *Phoenicurus ochruros* 14 cm 5½ in. Found on rocky ground and cliffs; also in towns, especially around factories. Constantly flicks its tail. Nests in holes in rocks and walls, and on buildings.

Nightingale *Luscinia megarhynchos* 16 cm 6½ in. Hides away among undergrowth in woods, and in thickets and hedges, sometimes around gardens. Nest concealed near ground. Very difficult to spot, but musical song can often be heard, especially at night (though other thrushes may also sing at night).

Robin *Erithacus rubecula* 14 cm 5½ in. Very often seen in woods, hedges, parks and gardens, hopping over the ground. Nests in holes in trees and walls. In Britain, robins are bold birds and often come to bird tables, but elsewhere in Europe they are shy. Robins are usually seen alone, or at most in pairs during spring and summer. They are so aggressive towards each other that they will even mistake their own reflection for another bird and attack it.

Wheatear

Stonechat

Whinchat

Redstart

Black Redstart

Nightingale

Robin

WARBLERS, GOLDCRESTS AND FLYCATCHERS

Warblers are small birds that flit about among trees, bushes and reeds, restlessly searching for insects to eat. They are named after their warbling songs, which vary widely from one species to another. The birds are often shy and difficult to spot. Most have dull colours with no obvious marks to give away their identity. Goldcrests are active little birds that flit through bushes and trees, hunting for insects. In the winter, they may join flocks of tits seeking food. The aptly named flycatchers are most likely to be seen sitting watchfully on a perch and then suddenly darting out to capture a fly or some other flying insect or swooping down to the ground to make a catch there. They often return to the same perch to wait for the next meal.

WARBLERS
Family Sylviidae

Grasshopper Warbler

white form

yellow form

Reed Warbler

Dartford Warbler

female   male

Blackcap

Garden Warbler

Sedge Warbler

Reed Warbler *Acrocephalus scirpaceus* 13 cm 5 in. Lives and nests among reeds and low bushes beside water and sometimes in fields. Perches on reed to sing, and suspends nest among reeds.

Grasshopper Warbler *Locustella naevia* 13 cm 5 in. Hides away and nests among dense undergrowth, long grass and reeds in marshes, and in more open country with scattered trees and bushes. Named after the grasshopper-like whirring sound of its song. The underparts may be white or yellowish.

Sedge Warbler *Acrocephalus schoenobaenus* 13 cm 5 in. Lives and nests among reeds, low bushes and hedges, usually near water; also among crops. Sings from perch at top of reed, and also during short flights.

Dartford Warbler *Sylvia undata* 13 cm 5 in. Lives and nests among low bushes, especially gorse, and heather on dry open ground and hillsides. Very shy, but may sing in flight. Has generally spread its breeding range during last few years, but could be on verge of extinction in Britain, partly due to cold winters and heath fires in hot summers.

Blackcap *Sylvia atricapilla* 14 cm 5½ in. Lives and nests among undergrowth, bushes and hedges in woods, parks and gardens. Usually shy, but may come to bird tables in winter. Only the male has a black cap; the female has a brown cap.

Garden Warbler *Sylvia borin* 14 cm 5½ in. Hides away and nests among undergrowth in woods and among thickets, hedges and bushes, often in parks and gardens. The plainest of all European birds; has no special markings.

Grasshopper Warbler   Reed Warbler   Sedge Warbler   Dartford Warbler   Blackcap   Garden Warbler

Willow Warbler

Lesser Whitethroat

Chiffchaff

Whitethroat

male

female

Whitethroat *Sylvia communis* 14 cm 5½ in. Lives and nests among low bushes, hedges and brambles around woods and in fields, also in gardens. Very active, darting in and out of cover and making short flights, singing while in the air.
Lesser Whitethroat *Sylvia curruca* 13 cm 5 in. Hides away and nests among bushes and trees in woods, parks and gardens.

Chiffchaff *Phylloscopus collybita* 11 cm 4½ in. Found in same places and as restless as willow warbler, but prefers areas with trees. Nests above ground. Virtually identical to willow warbler, except for song.
Wood Warbler *Phylloscopus sibilatrix* 13 cm 5 in. Lives and nests among woods and forests. Very active, singing as it moves through the leaves and flies from tree to tree.
Willow Warbler *Phylloscopus trochilus* 11 cm 4½ in. Found scurrying and flitting about in woods, among scattered trees and bushes, and in parks and gardens. Usually nests on the ground among bushes. Virtually identical to chiffchaff, except for song.

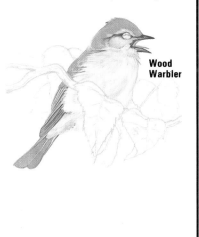

Wood Warbler

Whitethroat

Lesser Whitethroat

Chiffchaff

Wood Warbler

Willow Warbler

GOLDCRESTS

Family Regulidae

Goldcrest *Regulus regulus* 9 cm 3½ in. Found in woods and forests, especially in conifer trees; also in hedges, low bushes and undergrowth in winter. Builds basket-like nest of moss, often hung in conifer tree or among ivy.

female

Goldcrest

male

Goldcrest

FLYCATCHERS

Family Muscicapidae

Pied Flycatcher

female (and male in autumn)

male (summer)

Spotted Flycatcher

Spotted Flycatcher *Muscicapa striata* 14 cm 5½ in. Found at the edges of woods, among scattered trees, and in parks, orchards and gardens. Nests on buildings and tree trunks, often behind creepers. Flicks its tail as it perches. Only young birds are spotted; the adults are lightly streaked instead.
Pied Flycatcher *Ficedula hypoleuca* 13 cm 5 in. Found in woods, parks and gardens. Nests in hole in tree or wall, also in nest boxes. Flicks tail, but does not often return to same perch after chasing insects.

Spotted Flycatcher

Pied Flycatcher

TITS, NUTHATCHES AND TREECREEPERS

Tits are mainly woodland birds, but several are frequent visitors to gardens. They can be told apart from other common woodland and garden birds as they have chunky rounded bodies. In woods, they flit through the branches and hang from twigs to get at insects, buds and seeds; they nest in holes in trees, laying at least four or five eggs and sometimes as many as twenty. Tits can easily be attracted to a garden; they are bold birds and show little fear of man. Their agility enables them to feed easily at bird tables and to take food hung from a branch.

Babblers get their name from their constant chatter. Nuthatches are very agile tree birds, and are to be seen clambering up or running headfirst down trunks and along branches, picking insects from the bark. Wallcreepers climb over rock faces as well as walls, looking more like treecreepers than nuthatches. They also flutter through the air like butterflies. Treecreepers are named after the way they creep up tree trunks, seeking insects in the bark. They nest in holes and crevices in trees and behind ivy.

TITS
Family Paridae

Great Tit

Blue Tit

Coal Tit

Crested Tit

Willow Tit

Marsh Tit

Great Tit *Parus major* 14 cm 5½ in. Very often seen in woods, parks and gardens. Often pecks through milk bottle tops to reach the cream.

Blue Tit *Parus caeruleus* 11 cm 4½ in. Very often seen in woods, parks and gardens. Like great tit, it often opens milk bottles. Blue tits also tear strips from wallpaper, books and newspapers, an activity thought to be an extension of their habit of tearing bark from trees to find insects.

Coal Tit *Parus ater* 11 cm 4½ in. Common in woods, especially pine woods. Less often seen in gardens than great tit or blue tit.

Crested Tit *Parus cristatus* 11 cm 4½ in. Usually found in woods, especially among coniferous trees. Rarely seen in gardens.

Marsh Tit *Parus palustris* 11 cm 4½ in. Common in woods and often found in gardens. In spite of its name, it does not usually frequent marshes. Nests in natural holes in walls or trees.

Willow Tit *Parus montanus* 11 cm 4½ in. Common in woods, usually in damp places. Excavates nesting hole in rotten wood.

Great Tit	Blue Tit	Coal Tit	Crested Tit	Marsh Tit	Willow Tit

LONG-TAILED TITS
Family Aegithalidae

Long-tailed Tit *Aegithalos caudatus* 14 cm 5½ in. Found among bushes, thickets and hedges in woods, farmland and sometimes parks and gardens. Builds delicate globe-shaped nest with tiny entrance hole. The parent bird has to fold its long tail over its back when it is inside the nest.

Long-tailed Tit

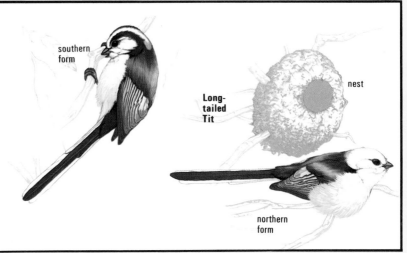

BABBLERS
Family Timaliidae

Bearded Tit or **Reedling** *Panurus biarmicus* 16 cm 6½ in. Lives among reeds; seen in flocks during winter. Gets its name from the large moustache marking of the male bird.

NUTHATCHES AND WALLCREEPERS
Family Sittidae

Nuthatch *Sitta europaea* 14 cm 5½ in. Lives in woods, parks and gardens; may visit bird tables. Nests in hole in tree, often plastering up entrance hole with mud. Two colour forms occur: birds with a white underside in northern Europe (*Sitta europaea europaea*), and birds with a buff underside elsewhere (*Sitta europaea caesia*). In Yugoslavia, Greece and Turkey, the very similar rock nuthatch (*Sitta neumayer*) may be seen climbing rock faces.

Wallcreeper *Tichodroma muraria* 16 cm 6½ in. Lives on mountain slopes, among gorges and cliffs; descends to valleys and foothills in winter, when it may be seen on buildings. Nests in rock cavities.

TREECREEPERS
Family Certhiidae

Treecreeper *Certhia familiaris* 13 cm 5 in. Found in woods, parks and gardens. Often seen with tits in winter. **Short-toed Treecreeper** *Certhia brachydactyla* 13 cm 5 in. Lives in same places as treecreeper. In central and southern Europe, this species is usually found at low altitude, whereas the treecreeper often prefers the mountains here.

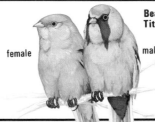

SHRIKES, ORIOLES AND CROWS

Shrikes are like small birds of prey. They perch in a tree or on a pole or wires, or they glide or hover over a hedge. As soon as a likely victim is spotted – a juicy insect, mouse or small bird – the shrike darts after it and snaps it up in its hooked beak. The victim is then usually taken to the shrike's 'larder', a sharp thorn or barbed wire fence where it is impaled so that the shrike can tear it apart.

Most orioles are brightly coloured birds of tropical forests. Only one species is found as far north as Europe. Crows are the largest perching birds and they are among the cleverest of all birds. They search boldly for all kinds of food, and open snails by dropping them on to a stone. They may also store food for the winter.

SHRIKES

Family Laniidae

Great Grey Shrike *Lanius excubitor* 24 cm 9½ in. Found at edges of woods, among scattered trees and bushes and in hedges and orchards. Nests in trees and bushes.

Red–backed Shrike *Lanius collurio* 18 cm 7 in. Found in bushy places and among brambles and thickets. Nests in bushes and small trees.

male
female
Red-backed Shrike
Great Grey Shrike

Red-backed Shrike
Great Grey Shrike

ORIOLES

Family Oriolidae

Golden Oriole

male
female
Golden Oriole

Golden Oriole *Oriolus oriolus* 24 cm 9½ in. Found in woods and orchards, and among trees in parks. Usually hides among leaves in tree tops.

CROWS

Family Corvidae

Carrion Crow

Rook

Carrion Crow *Corvus corone corone* 46 cm 18 in. Found on moors, at coasts and in fields, parks and gardens. Often seen alone or in pairs, and pairs nest alone in trees or on cliffs. Usually simply called crow rather than carrion crow.

Rook *Corvus frugilegus* 46 cm 18 in. Found in fields surrounded by lines of trees or small woods, in which it nests in colonies called rookeries. Also at seashore and open ground in winter. Usually seen in groups, often by motorways.

Raven *Corvus corax* 63 cm 25 in. Lives on sea cliffs and crags, in woods and open country, especially in hills and mountains and usually far from towns and villages. Builds huge nest on rock ledge or in tree. Often makes acrobatic display in the air, especially in spring. Hunts animals such as rabbits, hedgehogs and rats, but usually eats dead animals. The largest all-black bird found in Europe.

Chough *Pyrrhocorax pyrrhocorax* 38 cm 15 in. Lives in mountains and on cliffs by sea; may also be found in quarries. Nests on ledges and in caves and crevices. Often performs aerobatics in flight.

Magpie *Pica pica* 46 cm 18 in. Found in fields and open country with scattered trees and bushes, in which it builds a large dome-shaped nest. Often seen in town parks and gardens. May steal bright objects, and store them in its nest. It has a characteristic pattern of flight, in which it intermittently glides and then rapidly flaps its wings.

Nutcracker *Nucifraga caryocatactes* 33 cm 13 in. Lives in mountain forests, usually among conifer trees. Feeds mainly on nuts, which it may store in the autumn and find months later, even under snow.

Jay *Garrulus glandarius* 36 cm 14 in. Found in woods and orchards, and sometimes in town parks and gardens. Fond of acorns, which it stores for the winter by burying them in the ground. Can hold as many as six acorns in its mouth. It is a very lively and active bird and often flicks its tail. Its call is a harsh and noisy squawk.

Jackdaw *Corvus monedula* 33 cm 13 in. Found in fields and open country and at rocky coasts, nesting in holes in trees and rocks. Also seen on farms, and in towns and villages, where it nests in old buildings. Usually seen in flocks, walking jerkily or flying acrobatically.

Hooded Crow *Corvus corone cornix* 46 cm 18 in. Found in same places and lives in same way as carrion crow. Belongs to same species as carrion crow, and interbreeds with it in places where their ranges overlap, producing birds intermediate in appearance between them.

Raven

Jay

Chough

Magpie

Nutcracker

Hooded Crow

Jackdaw

Magpie   Nutcracker

Raven   Carrion Crow   Hooded Crow   Rook   Jackdaw   Jay   Chough

WRENS AND RELATIVES

All but one of the tiny members of the wren family live in America. Waxwings are unusual because except when nesting, they continually wander in flocks from place to place, looking for food. Another unusual group of birds are the dippers. Unlike other perching birds, they can swim and dive, and may even walk along the bottom of a stream to look for small freshwater animals. Accentors are small birds that root about on the ground seeking insects and spiders to eat, and also seeds in winter.

WRENS
Family Troglodytidae

Wren

Wren *Troglodytes troglodytes* 10 cm 4 in. Lives among low plants almost anywhere, from mountains, coasts and moors to woods, fields, parks and gardens. Often seen scurrying about in a flower bed or along the bottom of a hedge or wall, seeking insects among the litter on the ground. Nests in hedges and bushes and in holes in walls and trees.

Wren

WAXWINGS
Family Bombycillidae

Waxwing *Bombycilla garrulus* 18 cm 7 in. Found in woods, parks and gardens, busily eating berries and fruits. Nests in Arctic and spreads into Europe in winter in search of food. Every few years, too many waxwings are born and there is not enough food to go round. Great flocks then 'invade' southern and western Europe, reaching the British Isles, France, northern Italy and Yugoslavia.

Waxwing

Waxwing

DIPPERS
Family Cinclidae

Dipper

Dipper

Dipper *Cinclus cinclus* 18 cm 7 in. Lives by streams in mountains; may also be found by water at lower levels and at seashore in winter. Builds nest in river banks, under bridges or behind waterfalls.

ACCENTORS
Family Prunellidae

Dunnock

Dunnock

Dunnock or **Hedge Sparrow** *Prunella modularis* 15 cm 6 in. Found in woods, bushy countryside, hedges, parks and gardens, where it shuffles through flower beds. Resembles female house sparrow but is recognized by its narrow bill and dark grey head and underside. Nests in hedges, bushes and low plants.

STARLINGS
AND SPARROWS

Starlings like each other's company and live in flocks that in winter may contain thousands of birds. They wander over the ground, busily pecking here and there for food, and are probably the most frequent visitors to bird tables. They chatter constantly, often copying other sounds – even mechanical noises such as bells. Starlings build their rather untidy nests in a hole, usually in a tree or building.

No bird is better known than the house sparrow, which lives with man almost everywhere. Several other sparrows are also found in Europe and they too often seek man's company in urban environments and town gardens. Sparrows are small, streaky brown birds with stout bills, rather like several buntings (see page 39) but having special marks that are easy to recognize. They are most often seen in groups moving busily over the ground, pecking here and there for seeds.

winter

summer

Starling

STARLINGS

Family Sturnidae

Starling

Starling *Sturnus vulgaris* 21 cm 8½ in. Found throughout the countryside and also in towns, where flocks sleep on buildings and in trees. Nests in holes in trees or ground, on buildings and in nest boxes. As spring arrives, it loses the white spots of its winter plumage because the white tips of its feathers wear away. Also, the beak, which is dark in winter, turns yellow.

SPARROWS

Family Ploceidae

House Sparrow *Passer domesticus* 15 cm 6 in. Found in city centres and squares, parks and gardens, farms and fields. Nests under eaves, in holes in walls and rocks, and in nest boxes; also builds domed nest in creepers, bushes and trees. In Italy, Corsica and Crete, the Italian sparrow (*Passer domesticus italiae*) is found. It is a form of house sparrow with different head colours. It has a chestnut crown and white cheeks.

Tree Sparrow *Passer montanus* 14 cm 5½ in. Found in woods, among scattered trees and bushes, and in fields and gardens. Nests in holes in trees. Also lives and nests in towns and villages like house sparrow, especially in southern and eastern Europe.

Rock Sparrow *Petronia petronia* 14 cm 5½ in. Found in rocky and stony places; sometimes in gardens and among buildings. Nests in holes in rocks and trees.

Spanish Sparrow *Passer hispaniolensis* 15 cm 6 in. Found in woods and among scattered trees and bushes. Nests in trees and bushes, often in old nests of other birds. Less common in towns than house sparrow and tree sparrow.

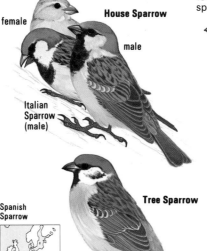

female

House Sparrow

male

Italian
Sparrow
(male)

Tree Sparrow

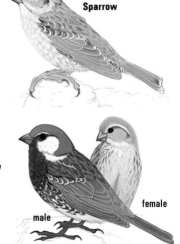

Rock Sparrow

female

male

Spanish Sparrow

House
Sparrow

Tree
Sparrow

Rock
Sparrow

Spanish
Sparrow

FINCHES AND BUNTINGS

Like tits, finches are generally among the most well-known and liked of birds, for they often come to gardens and parks, adding a touch of colour with their bright plumage. They usually appear in groups, working their way through trees or bushes or over low plants, as they search for seeds. They have stout beaks that can split open a seed as easily as a pair of nutcrackers.

Buntings are small, seed-eating birds like finches, and have similar stout bills to crack open seeds. Less well-known than finches, buntings are most likely to be seen feeding on the ground in winter, often in groups, and also singing from a perch in spring and summer.

Hawfinch

FINCHES

Family Fringillidae

Greenfinch *Carduelis chloris* 15 cm 6 in. Often seen among scattered trees and bushes, in fields, parks and gardens. Clings to net bags or wire baskets of nuts to feed, like tits. Nests in trees and bushes.

Hawfinch *Coccothraustes coccothraustes* 18 cm 7 in. Lives in woods, orchards, parks and gardens, but may hide away among leaves, especially in Britain. Nests in trees and bushes. Has huge bill that can crack open hard seeds.

Goldfinch *Carduelis carduelis* 13 cm 5 in. Lives and nests in same places as greenfinch, but does not come to feed on nuts. Often seen climbing over thistles or on high perch. Badly named, as gold is only seen clearly on wings in flight.

Siskin *Carduelis spinus* 12 cm 4¾ in. Found in woods, usually nesting in conifer trees and, in winter, feeding in alder and birch trees. Also seen in parks and gardens.

Linnet *Acanthis cannabina* 13 cm 5 in. Nests in low bushes, thickets and hedges, usually in open country but sometimes in parks and gardens. Roams over fields, rough pastures, and marshes in winter, sometimes in very large flocks.

Redpoll *Acanthis flammea* 13 cm 5 in. Usually found in woods, but may be seen in parks and gardens. Nests in trees and bushes; often seen in alder and birch trees in winter together with siskins. Scandinavian redpolls are light in colour.

male

female

Siskin

female

male

Redpoll

female

male

Greenfinch	Hawfinch	Goldfinch	Siskin

Linnet

Redpoll

male

female

Linnet

Goldfinch

Greenfinch

Bullfinch *Pyrrhula pyrrhula* 15 cm 6 in. Found in woods, orchards, hedges, parks and gardens. Nests in trees, bushes and hedges. Raids fruit trees for their buds.

Chaffinch *Fringilla coelebs* 15 cm 6 in. Often found in woods, among scattered trees and bushes, and in fields, hedges, orchards, parks and gardens. Nests in trees and bushes; spreads to more open country in winter.

Brambling *Fringilla montifringilla* 15 cm 6 in. Nests in trees in woods, and spreads to fields, parks and gardens in winter, often with chaffinches and other finches. Found especially in beech trees.

Crossbill *Loxia curvirostra* 16 cm 6½ in. Lives and nests among conifer (especially spruce) trees in woods and forests. The tips of its bill are crossed so that it can cut open fir cones to get at the seeds. When cones are scarce, it may spread in search of food, reaching the British Isles, France and Italy in great numbers.

BUNTINGS

Family Emberizidae

Corn Bunting *Emberiza calandra* 18 cm 7 in. Found in open fields and on rough ground with scattered bushes. Hides its nest in grass or low bushes. May be seen perching on a post, wall or telegraph wires.

Yellowhammer *Emberiza citrinella* 16 cm 6½ in. Found in clearings and at edges of woods, among scattered bushes, and in fields and hedges. Nests on the ground or in a low bush or hedge. Sings throughout spring and summer, repeating its famous phrase that seems to say 'little bit of bread and *no* cheese' – in fact, a group of short notes and a long one.

Snow Bunting *Plectrophenax nivalis* 16 cm 6½ in. Nests in crevices in rocks, usually high up in mountains. Spreads in winter to open coasts, hills and fields. Usually seen in winter in flocks known as snowflakes, from the way the little white birds seem to dance through the air.

Reed Bunting *Emberiza schoeniclus* 15 cm 6 in. Lives mainly in reed beds and swamps but also among bushes and hedges, where it nests on or near the ground. Spreads to fields in winter, and may come to bird tables in gardens.

INDEX